G000160295

PORT OF PLYMOUTH
SERIES

Millbay Docks

FORD

PORT OF PLYMOUTH SERIES

Millbay Docks

Martin Langley and Edwina Small

DEVON BOOKS

This book is part of a series which together form a history of the Port of Plymouth. Subject to demand it is hoped to publish, not necessarily in numerical order, the complete set of books comprising this project.

First published in Great Britain in 1987 by Devon Books

Copyright © Martin Langley & Edwina Small, 1987

ISBN: 0 86114-806-1

All rights reserved. No part of this publication may be reproduced, stored in a retrieval system, or transmitted in any form or by any means, electronic, mechanical, photocopying, recording or otherwise, without the prior permission of the copyright holder.

British Library Cataloguing-in-Publication Data
Langley, Martin
Millbay docks.—(Port of Plymouth series) .
1. Harbours—England—Plymouth (Devon)
2. Docks—England—Plymouth (Devon)
I. Title II. Small, Edwina III. Series 387.1'5 HE558.P5/

Printed and bound in Great Britain by A. Wheaton & Co. Ltd.

DEVON BOOKS

Official Publisher to Devon County Council
An imprint of Wheaton Publishers Ltd
A member of Maxwell Pergamon Publishing Corporation plc

Wheaton Publishers Ltd
Hennock Road, Marsh Barton, Exeter, Devon EX2 8RP
Tel: 0392 74121; Telex 42749 (WHEATN G)

SALES

Direct sales enquiries to Devon Books at the address above.
Trade sales to: Town & Country Books, P.O. Box 31, Newton Abbot, Devon TQ12 5AQ. Tel: 08047 2690

To
Captain Stan Daymond
former master of the tug *Boarhound*

Acknowledgements

Syd Beresford of West Hoe
Tom Bowden of Hartley
Jim Broad of Torpoint
J.F.O. Browning of West Hoe
Walter Crowther of West Hoe
Stan Daymond of Mutley
C.J. Low, M.B.E. of Ford Park
Bernard Mills of Beacon Park
A.M.S. Russell of Lymington
Tom Stroud of Higher Compton
Ronald Vosper of Crownhill
Bernard Y. Williams of London

British Transport Docks Board
Brittany Ferries
Guildhall Library, London
Plymouth Central Library
Titanic Historical Society, New York

Illustrations are reproduced by permission of the following:

Associated British Ports: pp. iii (map), 8,15;
S. V. Goodman: pp. 4,9,10,11;
Martin Langley: p.27;
Michael Parsons: p. 36;
Southampton City Museums: pp. 18,19;
Television South West: p. 37;
Western Morning News: pp. 14,24,25, 29,32.

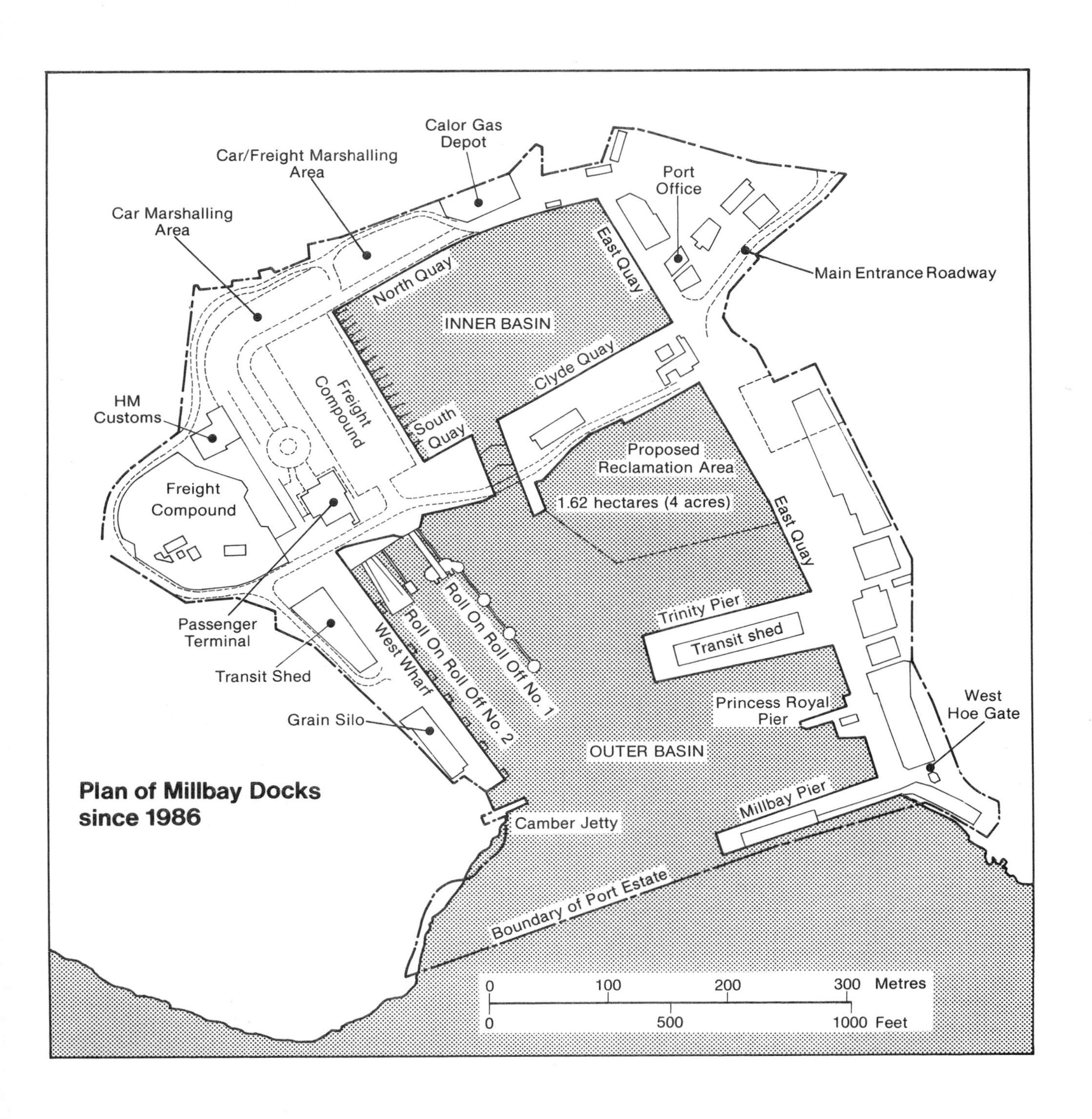

Plan of Millbay Docks since 1986

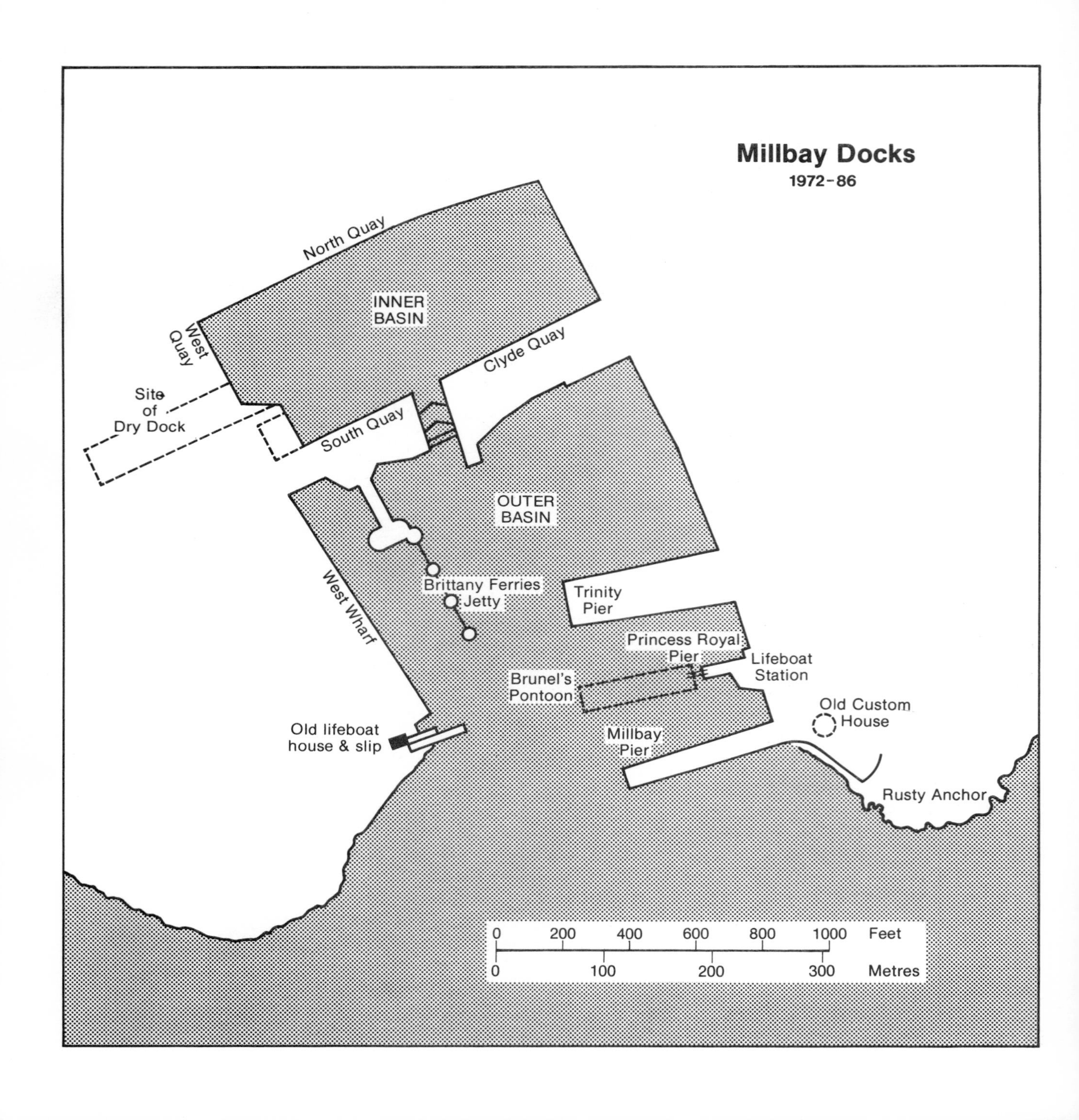
Millbay Docks
1972-86
North Quay
INNER BASIN
West Quay
Site of Dry Dock
South Quay
Clyde Quay
OUTER BASIN
West Wharf
Brittany Ferries Jetty
Trinity Pier
Princess Royal Pier
Lifeboat Station
Brunel's Pontoon
Old lifeboat house & slip
Millbay Pier
Old Custom House
Rusty Anchor
0 200 400 600 800 1000 Feet
0 100 200 300 Metres

Millbay Docks

EARLY HISTORY

'Millbay Docks,' wrote the *Illustrated London News* on 11 February 1857, 'is an undertaking which, at the cost of a quarter of a million pounds is calculated to promote the commercial interests of the Metropolis of the West, in a greater degree than any other enterprise which has marked the history of Plymouth.' It is fair to say that this prophecy was fulfilled before the turn of the century and that Millbay Docks, the last of Plymouth's inner harbours to be developed, have been the most successful.

The original Millbay Creek was much more extensive than the present dock area and encompassed also the Sourepool, a marshy, brackish lake which extended roughly along the line of today's Union Street, as far as Derry's Roundabout. Although in those earlier times Millbay was no rival to Sutton Pool, it was certainly used by shipping, and anchors have been dug up in the Octagon area. In the sixteenth century there were grist mills in Millbay owned by Sir Francis Drake. They were driven by the waters of his Dartmoor leat, which discharged into Millbay approximately where the angle between North and East quays is today. The Sourepool was drained ('made drie for a meadow') in 1592, reducing the creek to an area of about 45 acres.

Millbay first assumed importance to Plymouth during the Civil War, when for four years (1642 – 6) the port was subjected to a series of sieges and blockades. Forts at Oreston and Batten effectively closed the Cattewater and Sutton Harbour to supply ships, and the approach to Stonehouse Pool was threatened by the guns of Mount Edgcumbe. Only Millbay was out of range of the Royalist artillery, and thus it became, while the siege lasted, the harbour of Plymouth. Thereafter until the mid-eighteenth century Millbay retained its rural aspect: it was a quiet anchorage without jetties or port facilities. At the seaward end it was defended by small forts of Henry VIII's reign, and at the north-east corner were the tidemills which in 1695 were converted into a prison.

In 1756 the engineer John Smeaton established a workyard in Millbay for fashioning the stonework being assembled for the building of the third

Radford Road bridge, with rail track, over Gill's canal, by which his stone-carrying barges passed from West Hoe Quarry to Millbay Docks. Scene c.1855.

Eddystone Lighthouse. A jetty was built for unloading the ships bringing heavy loads of stone from Portland and Falmouth, and timber rails were laid in for the four-wheeled flat trucks used to shift the masonry. The tracks were 3 ft 6 in. gauge and connected by turntable. A former Dutch herring-boat, the *Neptune Buss*, was equipped here as a floating workshop and accommodation vessel before being moored off the Eddystone. A 10 ton craft named *Eddystone Boat* was based at Millbay and carried the stones to the reef as required; she took out the 2¼ ton foundation stone on the morning of Sunday, 12 June 1756. Here also were moored the purpose-built yawls which ferried the men and tools to and fro. The Millbay workyard was under the supervision of Josias Jessop, shipwright and Smeaton's right-hand man, who had two companies of men working alternately on the reef and at Millbay. The companies, under foremen named Richardson and Hill, each consisted of six masons, six labourers and boat crews. The work was completed and the lighthouse lit for the first time on 16 October 1759. The site of Smeaton's base was in the south-west corner of Millbay, where the Admiralty Boatyard now occupies the seaward end of West Wharf.

> Before the *Great Britain* made her appearance, the *Severn,* Cork steam-vessel, took on board from Gill's Military Pier a large party, and went out to meet her . . . The *Severn* followed the *Great Britain* into Millbay, firing salutes at intervals.
>
> *EXETER FLYING POST,*
> *19 June 1845*

DOCK DEVELOPMENT

The first we know of dock construction at Millbay appears in a map of the late 1830s where 'Union Dock' is shown between Martin and Phoenix Streets. The owners were B. and D. Derry and J. Meadows Rendel. When the Great Western Railway docks were later established in 1846, their rights were protected by a clause in the Act. No trace of the Union Dock remains today.

It was in 1840 that the most significant step was taken in the development of Millbay Creek. In that year an Act was passed granting Thomas Gill, owner of the West Hoe Estate, authority to erect a pier and works at the mouth of Millbay, deepen the bed of the creek and make any necessary excavations. Gill was quarrying away the west end of the Hoe Cliff at that time and had built small quays (where the Ocean Terminal building now stands) to serve his quarry, which is now West Hoe Park. The pier he was authorized to build became known as Millbay Pier. It was 500 ft long and was completed in 1844. The S.S. *Great Britain* berthed here during her maiden voyage in 1845 and was visited by 15 000 sightseers.

In 1846 the Great Western Dock Company was established by Act of Parliament to take over Millbay Pier and develop docks with full facilities for shipping. The great I. K. Brunel, engineer of the Great Western, South Devon and Cornwall railways, was engaged to design the new docks, and while capital was being raised for his plans to be implemented, the building of

The G.W.R.'s cross-channel steamer* Antelope *which, with her sister* Lynx, *ran a passenger-and-cargo service between Millbay Docks and Brest from 1908 – 11. Seen here at Trinity Pier.

wharves and warehouses adjoining Millbay Pier continued. Coastal shipping was now making regular use of the pier, especially passenger and cattle traffic from Ireland. Meanwhile Thomas Gill had excavated a small dock in his West Hoe quarry, where lighters could load with stone blocks and lime from the kilns. A short cut, or canal, provided connection with Millbay Docks, passing under a footbridge in Radford Road, and entering the Docks about 130 yards north of Millbay Pier. Nothing can be seen of this canal today. Having thus ensured the outlet for his stone, Gill sold Millbay Pier to the new Dock Company, of which he had become a director.

PACKET STATION

Gill was also chairman of the South Devon Railway, which reached Plymouth in 1848, Millbay Terminus being completed in 1849. It is not surprising therefore that Millbay was the first of Plymouth's inner harbours to get a rail connection with the main line. The extension from Millbay

The steamer* Melmore *discharging French strawberries from Plougastel, Brittany in June 1908, by steam crane at Millbay's West Wharf. Plymothians could obtain G.W.R. police passes to buy crates of fruit at the quayside.

Terminus was laid in 1850, the track bridging Gill's quarry canal and being carried as far as Millbay Pier. That same year the pier was granted Customs facilities and the octagonal Custom House built at the West Hoe entrance, to the designs of Wightwick and Damant; also the Pier Hotel was completed and railway passenger waiting-rooms provided. Furthermore, Millbay Docks were recognized as a government mail packet station, and the first mails were embarked in 1850. This was the occasion, Whitfeld tells us, for brass bands and general rejoicing, while the directors of the Screw Steam Navigation Company entertained the Mayor and corporation at a banquet.

At the request of the Irish Steamship Company, whose vessels were calling regularly, Brunel provided another pier in the form of an iron floating pontoon. This was 300 ft long by 40 ft wide, and was designed to hold 4000 tons of steam coal for bunkering. (After doing duty for more than a hundred years, in the 1960s the pontoon was towed a short distance away for breaking up. This proved more difficult than anticipated and the remains of the pontoon can be seen today north of Trinity Pier.) The regular berthing of steamers at the pontoon, together with the building, later, of the dam, somewhat inhibited the free passage of lighters from Gill's quarry. As a result West Hoe Basin was built to ship the stone away, and a light railway was laid down from the quarry through a tunnel, and through what were once the Reading Rooms and the Baths (today the premises of the Royal Western Yacht Club), on the quayside of the basin. The disused tunnel still exists and senior Plymothians will recall the old hand-cranked wooden cranes used for loading the stone. They could be seen, in various stages of disrepair, until the late 1930s. The canal and quarry dock were filled in by 1860.

A fatal accident occurred yesterday morning at the Great Western Docks on board the steamship *Genova,* while a gang of dock-labourers were shipping some casks of provisions on board. Thomas Weaving was employed in stowing the casks in the hold when another cask was allowed to roll off from the end of the brow and fell into the hold upon him, instantly crushing him to death.
WESTERN MORNING NEWS,
19 July 1865

BRUNEL'S PLANS TAKE SHAPE

Meanwhile, after delay due to financial anxieties, Brunel's work force had set to with a will. An earthen dam was built across the creek about 200 yards north of Millbay Pier, and behind this dam the inner basin was constructed, 1250 ft by 400 ft, of limestone and granite walls. The water area was 13 acres and the depth 22 ft. The length of the quay walls was 3490 ft and the wharfage area more than 15 acres. (The old Union Dock was filled in during the course of this work.) The entrance was 80 ft wide and dock gates (making the inner basin independent of tides) had a depth on the sill of 10 ft 3 in. at LWOST. Opening from the basin at the west end was a graving dock, 367 ft long by 92 ft, with wide gates to admit paddle steamers. The original 1851 specification for the docks, which still exists, includes details of the Pump House which stood on the south side, for emptying the graving dock. When the earth dam was removed, about 400 ft of it was left *in situ* on the east side to facilitate the building of Trinity Pier. Fine warehouses were built on the quay behind Trinity and Pontoon piers. The inner basin was opened informally in February 1857 by taking in an 1100 ton vessel for repairs. Over the years that followed a few modifications were made to Brunel's original works: in 1878 West Wharf deepwater berth was constructed and Trinity Pier enlarged; in 1902 the inner basin entrance was repositioned further west and new lock gates, hydraulic equipment and a swing bridge installed; in 1903 Millbay Pier was lengthened. No other significant constructional changes took place until the creation of the Roscoff Ferry Terminal in 1973 – 4.

LIFEBOAT STATION

In 1862 the Royal National Lifeboat Institution established a new station for Plymouth in the south-west corner of Millbay Docks. A temporary lifeboat house costing £159 and a 130 ft launching slip were built on a site now covered by the transit sheds of West Wharf. A more substantial lifeboat house was erected in 1897 and was in use until 1926, when the pulling-and-sailing boat was replaced by a long-awaited motor lifeboat. Since then Plymouth lifeboats have been kept afloat at moorings in the outer basin. The headquarters building is on Princess Royal Pier.

> Twenty-five deported passengers from the United States and 5 'removals' who had been helped by the American Government to return to this country, were among those landing at Plymouth yesterday from the 'President Harding'.
> *WESTERN MORNING NEWS, 2 August 1935*

SHIPBUILDING

Marine and general engineers, who tendered also for shipbuilding, set up business in the docks: Ellacott & Son (1871 – 1921) at East Quay, Bickle & Co. Ltd (1887 – 1958) south of the graving dock, and Willoughby Bros Ltd (1857 – 1969) beside the graving dock. A significant amount of shipbuilding was carried on. Willoughby's built vessels for the Royal Mail Steamship Company, Customs and Excise, the War Department and other patrons, and chain ferries for the passages at Torpoint, Saltash, Littlehampton and Felixstowe. Many men who served their time as fitters at Willoughby's went on to become chief engineers of ocean-going ships. The graving dock, where Willoughby's accepted vessels for Board of Trade surveys, refitting and extensive repairs, soon proved to be a major asset of the port. Fuelling facilities were provided in the outer basin and by 1857 Millbay was one of the principal coaling stations in the English Channel.

PASSENGERS AND FREIGHT

The Docks steadily established themselves, both passenger and freight traffic being on the increase, for larger vessels could be handled than at Sutton Pool. Packet steamers and coastal liners called on regular timetable services, and in addition to carrying the Royal Mails and miscellaneous cargoes, had limited

The Dutch freighter S.S. *Celaeno* ***(3544 tons, 1916) of Rotterdam discharging grain by hydraulic cranes at West Wharf in April 1926. In those pre-silo days the king's harbourmaster's house and signal yards were prominent.***

passenger accommodation. Comfortable cabins could be reserved at each line's Plymouth office, or from their local agents. By the turn of the century Plymothians living near the docks or the Hoe could see from their windows the Liverpool boat depart on Monday mornings, followed by the London boat at 6p.m. In midweek there was a sailing to Belfast, and another boat for London on Fridays. Steamers of the British & Irish Steam Packet Co., the Clyde Shipping Co. and others worked regularly in and out of Millbay Docks. A wide range of freight was handled over the years, with grain always a principal import. All this activity, however, was eclipsed by the ocean liner traffic which began in 1873 and lasted for ninety years, reaching its peak in 1930.

The tender** Palmerston, **bearing the letters G.W.R. on her funnel, taking passengers from the 12 500 ton White Star liner** Persic **to meet the boat train at Millbay, c.1910.

OCEAN TERMINAL

In the 1870s the big steamship lines were making Plymouth the first port for disembarkation on the eastward route from America. Entry to England via Plymouth became known to Americans as 'the route which cuts the corners off', and it represented a saving of a day or more on the journey. There was no question of berthing: the ocean liners anchored in the Sound or Cawsand Bay and it was soon clear that purpose-built tenders were needed to serve them. The railway was the obvious chief beneficiary of such a service, and took the initiative in ordering the first of the steamers which were to run throughout the next ninety years from Millbay Docks.

THE EARLIER LINER TENDERS

This steamer was the *Sir Francis Drake*, an iron paddler of 173 tons built by Allsup's of Preston and delivered in 1873. Initially she was owned jointly by the West Cornwall Railway Committee and the Plymouth Great Western Docks Co., but she was transferred to the Great Western Railway under the G.W.R. and South Devon Railway Amalgamation Act in 1878. She was certificated for excursion work and pioneered the coastal pleasure trips on which the Millbay tenders were employed in summer when not serving the liners. A consort was provided when the iron paddler *Sir Walter Raleigh*, a slightly smaller tender (151 tons), was delivered by the same builders three years later. Her lower passenger capacity proved an inconvenience as the liner trade boomed, and she was sold to South Shields in 1895 after nineteen years, whereas most of the tenders served over thirty, and some more than forty, years.

Two more tenders were acquired in 1883, one second-hand, the other new and purpose-built. The paddler *Palmerston* (109 tons) was nearly twenty years old and had been working as a tug/tender in Dover harbour. She served thirty

Ugly duckling: the 387 ton paddle tender *Cheshire,* ***ex-Mersey ferry, came to Millbay in 1905. Believed sold for scrap in 1913 after a stranding, she is seen here returning from a calling liner with mail.***

years at Millbay and was sold to Newcastle in 1913. The *Smeaton* (369 tons) was an iron twin-screw vessel and set the pattern for future construction – squat and broad in the beam, with a large funnel. She was destined to be the longest-serving tender at Plymouth, with an eventual forty-seven years to her credit when she was finally sold to Belfast. The next arrival, in 1891, was the iron twin-screw steamer *Sir Richard Grenville* (420 tons), built by Laird's of Birkenhead. She survived requisitioning in the Great War and served forty years at Millbay before being sold in 1931. In 1901 the London & South Western Railway opened their Ocean Terminal at Stonehouse Pool and the Great Western boats at Millbay thereafter operated to some extent in circumstances of competition rather than monopoly for eighteen years. A reversion to paddle propulsion was made in 1905, when the 387 ton *Cheshire* came from Birkenhead to augment the fleet. She was a former Mersey ferry. After eight years at Plymouth she was sold to Hamburg to be scrapped but was wrecked on the Friesian Islands while on passage.

The Later Liner Tenders

In 1908 the first of two steel twin-screw sisters, the *Sir Francis Drake*, arrived from Cammell Laird's at Birkenhead. The original *Sir Francis Drake*, now thirty-five years old, was thereupon renamed *Helper* and relegated to reserve vessel until sold two years later. No doubt the name was appropriate but it contrasted oddly with those of the Elizabethan heroes. The other sister, the *Sir Walter Raleigh*, worked for a year at Fishguard before coming to Millbay.

The competition with the Stonehouse Ocean Terminal had eased under a convention by which the South Western handled the Transatlantic passenger traffic while the Great Western carried the mails. Stonehouse Pool Terminal, however, closed down in 1911 and the smaller of the two steam tenders there, the *Atalanta*, was aquired by the G.W.R. and brought to Millbay. She was retained for twelve years, though for the earlier part of this time she worked at Fishguard. In 1923 she was sold to the Royal Mail Steam Packet Co. In 1929 a new steel twin-screw tender, the *Sir John Hawkins* (939 tons) arrived as replacement for the ageing *Smeaton* . Arguably the most handsome of the screw tenders, the *Hawkins* was also the largest and was capable of about 14 knots. The year after her arrival the liner traffic reached its highest-ever figure, 788 liner calls being made at Plymouth in 1930, three or four liners sometimes

The tender Sir Richard Grenville **(1) which served Millbay from 1891 – 1931. With the arrival of the oil-fired** Sir Richard Grenville **(2) she was renamed** Penlee **and sold later that year.**

There is no passenger activity to be seen in this picture of the tender Smeaton ***at Millbay Pier, with ocean mails coaches standing at the terminal, c.1920.***

Sir Walter Raleigh **(2) landing ocean mails at Millbay Docks by electric-belt conveyor for a 'Castle'-hauled express, about 1926.**

arriving in a day. All the great companies used Plymouth, and the names of the famous vessels which the tenders served between the wars read like a page from some 'Burke's Peerage of the sea': *Mauretania, Aquitania, Berengaria, Olympic, Paris, Ile de France, Leviathan, Bremen, Normandie* and *Queen Mary*. In addition to handling passengers, baggage and mails, the tenders could carry up to four cars. Retired Chief Engineer Tom Stroud recalls that these were loaded by liner's crane on to the tender's foredeck and offloaded by a docks crane. A new tender was delivered by Earle's of Hull in 1931, the *Sir Richard Grenville* (901 tons). The old *Grenville* was renamed *Penlee* and sold to Dover a few months later. In spite of the considerable liner traffic, the tenders continued to run sea excursions which were well patronized, the most popular being to Looe and Fowey, and a cruise around the Eddystone Lighthouse. Embarkations were always at Millbay Docks.

The tenders were requisitioned by the government in the Second World War, *Sir John Hawkins* going north to Scapa Flow as an anti-aircraft-armed boom defence vessel. The war blew a chill wind over the liner traffic, which never again attained its former importance. A first result was the sale of the *Sir Walter Raleigh* to Southampton in 1947. Some of her fittings, including a

Christmas mail being manhandled on to Millbay Pier from the boat deck of the *Sir Richard Grenville* **(2), 1935.**

named lifebuoy, are today displayed in the Great Western Railway Museum at Swindon. The other three tenders, now transferred to the ownership of the British Transport Commission, were refitted and the sea excursions were resumed. But the demand for tenders fell year by year as the liner companies began to omit the call at Plymouth and in 1953 the *Sir Francis Drake* was withdrawn and scrapped the next year. In 1957 the number of liner calls had dropped to 154, and in 1961 the French line, the port's best customer, withdrew. The *Sir John Hawkins* was disposed of to Dutch shipbreakers the following May and the end of the liner traffic was now in sight. In October 1963 the *Sir Richard Grenville* was withdrawn and sold, and ninety years of handling liner traffic at Plymouth came to an end.

OCEAN MAILS SPEED RECORD

The ocean-liner era had been an important chapter in Plymouth's maritime history, and the heyday of Millbay Docks. Between 1879 and 1930 the number of passengers using the docks increased from 3538 to 43 072. In the peak year of 1930 passenger and mail services had called at Plymouth from over seventy different ports, thirty of the world's most important steamship lines being represented. A national by-product of the Plymouth liner calls was the setting up of a world railway speed record. It was in May 1904 that the Norddeutscher Lloyd liner *Kronprinz Wilhelm*, a 25 knot flier and former holder of the Blue Riband, left New York for Plymouth. Besides passengers and mails she carried

Tender alongside Princess Royal Pier discharging mail via electric belt conveyor straight into T.P.O. van of Ocean Mails express. A 1920s photograph of the ocean terminal.

Titanic **crew survivors at West Hoe Gate, Millbay Docks, 28 April 1912. Note Millbay Pier's overall roof, now demolished, the Wightwick-designed octagonal Custom House (left) and the Ocean Terminal building (right), now both disused and dilapidated.**

bullion – the U.S. payment to France for the Panama Canal. At 8 a.m. on 9 May the *Kronprinz Wilhelm* was at anchor in Plymouth Sound and the mails and bullion were being rapidly offloaded into the tenders. Eighty-three minutes later the tenders had docked at Millbay, mails and bullion had been transferred to the train and the Ocean Mails Express was leaving the docks for London. The engine, no. 3440 *City of Truro*, was hauling five coaches and her driver was Moses Clements. There was an inspector on the footplate in anticipation of a very fast run. The train climbed from Totnes to Dainton tunnel at almost a mile a minute and running down from Whiteball Tunnel to Wellington the speed reached 102.3 m.p.h. Those were the days of the 'Great Way Round' via Bristol, and the train spent 3½ minutes there while the engine was changed. No. 3065 *Duke of Connaught* completed the run to Paddington at over 80 m.p.h. for most of the way. A journey time of 3 hours 47 minutes! Eighty years later today's diesel expresses do only marginally better!

TITANIC SURVIVORS

On Sunday, 28 April 1912, Millbay Docks were the scene of the return of most of the surviving crew of the *Titanic*, fourteen days after the White Star liner sank in the Atlantic. At 8 o'clock that morning the S.S. *Lapland* had anchored in Cawsand Bay with those 167 members of *Titanic's* crew aboard who had not been detained in New York for the American inquiry, and 1927 sacks of mail that had been scheduled to be carried by the *Titanic*. Three tenders went out from Millbay Docks to disembark passengers and mails. The third tender, the *Sir Richard Grenville*, carrying the *Titanic* crew survivors, cruised about the Sound killing time, while the dock labourers and porters, after clearing the first two tenders, were paid off and escorted outside the dock gates at West Hoe. It was not until after midday that the tender was given the signal that all was ready for her and she was allowed to berth at Millbay Pier. Thus, in an atmosphere of stealth and secrecy, were *Titanic's* crew survivors returned to their homeland. A special train later took them from Millbay Docks to Southampton, where their arrival after dark, at 10.10 p.m., was fully reported next day in a quite emotional and unrestrained article in the *Southampton Echo*.

THE *EGYPT'S* GOLD

During the early 1930s Millbay Docks were the base for the salvage of gold from the *Egypt*. This P. & O. liner had been sunk off the French coast in 1922 after collision with the cargo steamer *Seine*. An Italian salvage concern, Sorima, had been attempting since 1929 to recover the valuable cargo of gold

Surviving stewardesses from the *Titanic* **photographed on Millbay Pier.**

Stewards and cooks from the* Titanic *in temporary quarters at the Ocean Terminal, Plymouth.

The Italian salvage vessel Artiglio II ***returning to Plymouth with the first £180 000 of gold from the wreck of the*** Egypt, ***June 1932.***

and silver bars and boxes of sovereigns. Working from the port of Brest, the Sorima team had found the wreck and succeeded in cutting it open opposite the strong room, when winter gales forced them to abandon work for that year. They were working on the wreck of a munition ship in the Bay of Biscay when an explosion sunk their salvage ship *Artiglio* and killed many of their most skilled divers. Following this disastrous setback, Sorima acquired a newer and larger vessel, *Artiglio II*, and trained new divers by the following summer (1931). They also changed their base to Plymouth. In July and August that year they cut their way through to the strong room of the *Egypt*, but the weather broke for that season. The method they employed was to lower a diver in an observation chamber to a position over the wreck and then follow his telephoned instructions for placing explosives or lowering the grab. The depth of 71 fathoms was too great for divers working in standard dress.

In May 1932 *Artiglio II* sailed from Millbay Docks and took up position over the wreck once more. Up to this time the Italians had spent £150 000 on the work, having combed the seabed for two seasons to locate the wreck and blasted away at her for another two seasons to cut their way to the gold; but they were now to reap their reward. On 22 June the grab came dripping from the sea

An impression of the underwater scene as Artiglio II **worked on the sunken** Egypt. **A diver, in the observation chamber, has given directions for the lowering of the grab.**

clutching the first two gold bars! The bars came safely over the gunnel and thudded on to the deck. Then in three following days of good weather Sorima recovered £180 000 worth of gold, of which they were entitled to one half. Commendatore Quaglia, in charge of the operation, sent a message to Lloyd's and steamed for Plymouth. Among those who gathered at Millbay Docks to congratulate him were Sir Percy Mackinnon, Chairman of Lloyd's, and Sir Joseph Lowry, secretary of the Salvage Association.

On 27 June *Artiglio II* left Plymouth again, but adverse weather persisted throughout July, and it was the second week in August before the divers could resume work below. Within a few days they raised another £20 000 of treasure and this was landed at Millbay Docks on 14 August. Before the end of August another calm spell enabled them to bring up gold, silver and sovereigns to the value of £190 000. Yet another £70 000 worth was recovered before the end of the year and the *Artiglio II* then returned to Plymouth. In 1933 even better progress was made. Five lucky spells of fine weather enabled them to lift £206 000 worth of bullion. An unexpected calm spell as late as November saw another £8000 worth of gold raised from the wreck, all this treasure being landed at Millbay Docks. In the spring of 1934 *Artiglio II* steamed out to prepare for the final phase. Wreckage was cleared from the access to the strong-room and the grab went down into the widened hole. By the end of August the Sorima team recovered another £160 000 of treasure and in September a further £30 000. When weather brought diving to an end that year, a total of £1 183 000 had been raised, and *Artiglio II* left the scene for the last time. Never before had gold been recovered from so great a depth and the Italians' achievement was not surpassed until the raising of gold from H.M.S. *Edinburgh* in the Barents Sea in 1981.

MAKING HISTORY – IN PEACE AND WAR

Millbay Docks has played host to a number of historic vessels. We noted earlier the arrival of the S.S. *Great Britain* in 1845. A later visitor was the Research Ship *Discovery* in 1904, which had earned fame after four years in the Antarctic under Captain Scott. But at no time did the docks play a more significant part in the history of the port than during the Second World War, especially in the tense days of 1940. Joan Amos, whose husband Freddy later became Second Cox'n of Plymouth lifeboat, was one of many girl dockers who then worked at Millbay Docks. Living now at Peter Tavy she well recalls those stirring, dangerous and often tragic times. In May 1940 about 22 000 French soldiers evacuated at Dunkirk passed through the Docks within six days to board ships in the Sound and return to France. Each transport was played out to the strains of 'La Marseillaise'. Immediately after the disastrous fall of France the docks were

Aerial view of Millbay Docks, c.1927. Smeaton ***(nearer) and another tender (***Drake ***or*** Raleigh ***of 1908) lie at Brunel's pontoon. Note the railway coaches at the Ocean Terminal and cranes on Trinity Pier and Clyde Quay.***

Brittany Ferries' twin-screw M.V. *Cornouailles* ***(3383 tons, 1977), purpose-built for the Roscoff route, at the berthing dolphins in May 1977. She had just arrived at Plymouth, under the command of Captain Le Saux.***

again dealing with many thousands of returning British, Canadian and French troops, disembarking from every kind of transport from liner to trawler. In the days following the sinking of the *Lancastria* in Quiberon Bay on June 17, hundreds of survivors, many dreadfully burned, were landed at Millbay Docks and rushed to hospitals by a fleet of ambulances. By 23 June, the fourth evening after the evacuation of Brittany, there were eighty-four ships in Plymouth Sound and about 100 000 men had been entrained at Millbay Docks.

FREIGHT TRAFFIC

Between the wars, while the mail boats provided the glamour, freight traffic had become important and was increasing. Typical of life in the docks was this laconic notice taken at random from the *Western Morning News* of 6 February 1926: 'Millbay Docks — S.S. *City of Mandalay* discharged most of a cargo of 10 000 tons of barley'. A speciality was the handling of strawberries, broccoli and potatoes from Brittany in season. For the immediate pre-war year of 1938 the principal imports were shown as: wheat, maize, flour, barley, baltic timber, general merchandise and iron and steel manufactures. The total import figure was 192 064 tons. Exports have never been on the same scale but in 1938 were

Trawlers of the Scottish mackerel fleet at Millbay in January 1980. Their annual appearance is less than welcome to the local fishermen based on Sutton Harbour.

principally: general cargo, bunker coal, iron and steel manufactures, and flour. The total export figure was 35 436 tons. A typical post-war year was 1957 when imports totalled only 143 831 tons, and exports had diminished to 31 413 tons.

The Port of Plymouth's roll-on roll-off freight traffic increased by nearly 16% in 1984. The terminal handled more than 18,000 freight units last year and vessel calls were up 12% on last year.
WESTERN MORNING NEWS,
28 February 1985

BRITTANY CROSS-CHANNEL SERVICE

With the opening of the Brittany cross-Channel service in 1973, Millbay Docks became a popular route for continental vegetables and other freights. By 1977 309 000 tonnes of cargo were being handled, over 100 000 tonnes more than in 1972. The cargo was mostly lorry-borne, the juggernauts passing straight through Plymouth and thundering up the A38. Although begun primarily as a freight service, the Plymouth – Roscoff route became popular with passengers, 200 000 being carried by 1977, with three ships in use. In 1978 a further service was added, from Plymouth to Santander in northern Spain. The story of Brittany Ferries has therefore been a success story for Millbay Docks, and was made possible by the construction of a roll-on roll-off (Ro-ro) berth, built in 1971 – 2 at a cost of £1 million. It consists of three side-mooring dolphins and two stern-mooring dolphins. The two stern dolphins also carry support towers for the machinery which operates the vertical motion of the link-span bridge.

FISHING VESSELS

Millbay Docks are not associated in the public mind with deep-sea fishing, yet today it is quite usual to find a number of Channel Island trawlers at the quays. The fishing connection came about through the congestion of Sutton Pool in the late 1970s. The larger landings of fish due to modern methods, the opening up of European markets when Britain joined the E.E.C. and the arrival of continental boats to work from Plymouth, resulted in a larger fleet which was the cause of this congestion, and trawlers were diverted to Millbay to land their catches. The winter mackerel-fishing vessels which come down from Scotland each January are often too large for the Barbican space, so they also have to work from Millbay Docks. Most of the mackerel landed is exported, with small quantities being converted into fish meal. The docks are not licensed for a fish-market, and fishing vessels discharge direct to transport for pre-determined markets both within the United Kingdom and abroad.

S.S. *Duchess of Devonshire* ***keeping her annual date with the graving dock at Millbay for Board of Trade survey, April 1934. It was the last time: she was wrecked that August. In 1973 – 4 the dock was filled in and is now a car park.***

The calor gas tanks on North Quay, Inner Basin, with motor tanker *Sunny Girl* ***alongside.***

YACHTS AND EXCURSION SHIPS

Millbay has not neglected the leisure sailor: once the principal departure-point for sea-going excursion steamers, it now caters for yachtsmen at the main racing events. From the coming of the first liner tender in 1873 to the departure of the last in 1963, the railway steamers ran very popular sea excursions from Millbay Pier. The Millbrook Steamboat Co., which operated chiefly from the Promenade Pier off The Hoe, appropriately used Brunel's pontoon before the First World War for their 'crack' steamer which bore his name. The Devon Dock, Pier & Steamship Co.'s *Duke of Devonshire* and *Duchess of Devonshire*, of Exmouth, always berthed in Millbay when calling at Plymouth, and the *Duchess* was annually refitted by Willoughby's in the dry dock. In 1932 P. & A. Campbell Ltd based their 438 ton paddler *Westward Ho!* at Millbay, running as far east as Weymouth and west to Penzance, but

Industrial salt in bulk being discharged by grab for transport by road; an East Quay scene, 1979.

she was withdrawn before the Second World War. Today, sea excursions from Millbay are limited to the occasional visit of the preserved *Waverley*, working from Trinity Pier. Yachting, on the other hand, has boomed. Such events as the two-yearly Fastnet Race, the Single-handed Transatlantic Race and the Round Britain Race, crowd the inner basin with a fleet of yachts from all parts of the world.

WHARFAGE: INNER BASIN

The wharfage of Inner Basin consists of North, East, Clyde and South Quays. (A former West Quay is now covered by the freight compound.) On **North Quay** is a calor-gas storage plant, protected by an automatic sprinkler system, and holding about 870 tons of gas. The estimated annual turnover is about 5000 tons, and the installation is supplied by tankers from France, mostly Le Havre, with gas originally piped from Algeria. Road tankers carry out distribution from the docks.

East Quay was formerly occupied by Jewsons', timber merchants. They received seaborne soft woods in a rough state and cut and distributed them to their customers' requirements. A special lifting device called 'Plymouth Gear' or 'Pearce's Gear' was used in place of rope slings for discharging loose timber. 'It was,' says former docker Syd Beresford, 'a system of metal grips patented by Cyril Pearce, the chief Docks foreman. Its use was found to be both safer than rope slings and more efficient. It increased working speed from 30 to 65 standards per day.'

Clyde Quay is so named because it was here that the Clyde Shipping Co.'s vessels called, until October 1966. It is now used by occasional trawlers.

South Quay was formerly used for the discharge of coal from Blyth. Arrivals averaged one a month and the coal was discharged into the Co-op depot at the docks. When this berth was periodically dredged, the dredger crews often found the grab largely filled with spilled coal, and benefited accordingly! Scrap metal is sometimes exported to the iron-and-steel ports of Spain, Italy and The Netherlands, loading being by means of grabs and gravity chutes.

WHARFAGE: OUTER BASIN

The wharfage of the Outer Basin consists of East Quay, Trinity and Millbay Piers, the Ro-ro berth and West Wharf. **East Quay** (built in the late 1840s) has been long disused, despite its fine warehouses and former direct rail link. Berthed alongside are the rusting remains of Brunel's iron pontoon of 1852.

West Wharf (1878) is 900 ft long and has deep-water berths for 800 ft. Here is handled Millbay's principal import, grain, with an annual turnover of

Pearce's 'Plymouth gear' (which brought the inventor ½d. per standard moved) unloading timber at Clyde Quay in 1965, operated by dockers Victor Carter and Gordon Hoskins. Willoughby's building is in the right background.

Aerial view of the Docks, 1961. Soon to disappear were: Willoughby's dry dock (top left); Sir John Hawkins ***at Trinity Pier; Brunel's pontoon with*** Sir Richard Grenville ***alongside; and the Ocean Terminal buildings (centre foreground).***

about 75 000 tons. The grain is discharged at a rate of about 100 – 150 tons an hour by suction pumps into a large silo on the wharf and then processed in Spillers' Mill just outside the dock area.

Trinity and Millbay Piers are little used. The roof canopy at Millbay Pier (which once sheltered liner passengers boarding or leaving tenders) was dismantled in February 1972. Trinity Pier, at one time used by Coast Lines' boats for Ireland and Liverpool, formerly had hydraulic cranes for cargo work; these were later superseded by electric cranes, but now there are none.

OFFICIAL VESSELS

Over the years Millbay Docks have been the base for the launches of the Board of Trade, H.M. Customs and the Port Health Authority. They have traditionally been moored, with the Plymouth lifeboat, between Trinity Pier and the inner basin. The Board of Trade maintained a boat at Plymouth until 1930. The last, which served for nine years, was the paraffin-engined *Gadfly*. Whether her name was chosen as a whimsical reminder either of the gadfly's attributes of blood-sucking or of restless activity it was equally inappropriate, as in fact she seemed seldom to be away from her mooring! H.M. Customs have always maintained a Waterguard Office on Millbay Pier. Their present launch is the 25 ft *Kingfisher*, but the revenue cutters sometimes call in the course of their coastal patrols. The Port Health Authority launch was used for taking the doctor to incoming ships and (until 1932) acting as tender to the isolation ships in the Sound. The last launch, the 40 ft *Argus*, was sold in 1981.

> The Devonport frigate *Avenger* today escorted the 500 ton Panamanian motor vessel *Reeve* into Millbay Docks after a 12-hour rescue operation in heavy seas.
> *WESTERN EVENING HERALD, 10 December 1983*

RESEARCH VESSELS

From 1967 – 77 Millbay was a base for the ships of the National Environment Research Council. The stern trawler *Noblesse* was purchased from the White Fish Authority in 1966 and converted by Willoughby's of Millbay for oceanographic research. She was renamed *John Murray* after Professor J. Murray, F.R.S., the eminent marine biologist. After operating from Plymouth in the areas of the U.K. continental shelf, the North Atlantic and the Azores for four years she was transferred to Barry, Glamorgan, from where she carried out similar geological, geophysical and biological cruises until sold. *John Murray* was replaced at Plymouth by the *Shackleton*, a considerably larger vessel which had been working for the British Antarctic Survey and had to be converted for general purpose oceanographic research. The *Shackleton* operated from Millbay until 1976. Her successor was the 2000 ton *Discovery*, built in Aberdeen in 1962. Although also owned by the

Unloading citrus fruit by electric crane at Trinity Pier in 1970; seventy cranes are carried in each lift, using palette and wire strops.

(Right) ***Paper reels being hoisted from a freighter's forehold at Trinity Pier in 1974: there are nine reels in a lift, using purpose-designed flat strops. Geoff Beresford, signalling the crane driver, has since become a shop steward.***

P P L
30229

The tender *Sir Richard Grenville* **(2) in 1958, five years before the Millbay Ocean Terminal closed. Evening dances were sometimes held at sea on her broad decks.**

N.E.R.C. she was manned by the Royal Fleet Auxiliary and carried out research for the Institute of Oceanographic sciences. *Discovery*, however, has not used Plymouth as a base since 1977.

MILLBAY DOCKS TODAY

The disappearance of the orthodox freighter in favour of container ships, the collapse of ocean and coastal liner traffic, and the virtual extinction of sea excursions, combined to make ghost quays of much of Millbay's wharfage. Today only West Wharf and the ferryport dolphins berth are in constant regular use and the other quays, although often berthing trawlers or private craft, rarely handle cargo. However, the docks still offer ships safe twenty-four-hour access with lockfree entry at any state of the tide and Associated

Brittany Ferries' M.V. Kerisnel **on relief duty at Plymouth, turning in Millbay Docks.**

British Ports, who succeeded British Transport Dock Board as the controlling authority in 1984, have made a determined bid to enable Millbay to compete effectively both for passengers and freight.

The provision of modern facilities has involved reducing the water area by infilling at the south-western end of Inner Basin to accommodate a freight compound, while 4 acres are to be reclaimed in the north-eastern corner of Outer Basin to provide more operational and storage space. Following the £1 million investment in the dolphin berth for Brittany Ferries in 1972, a second Ro-ro berth was provided in 1986 at West Wharf – a £4½ million investment – able to accommodate vessels up to 180 m length and of 8.5 m draught. This meant that Brittany Ferries could operate a more frequent service to France and Spain. In addition there is now a CMB Trailship service to Bilbao, operated twice weekly by the M.V. *Kaprifol*. Cruise ships also use Millbay both as an embarkation point and as a popular centre for one-day stopovers. About 330 000 passengers pass through Millbay Docks every year, and large quantities of French and Spanish fruit and vegetables arrive on the Ro-ro services for distribution by motorway throughout Britain. Imaginative management has kindled new commercial life.

Excellent growth prospects are forecast for the Port of Plymouth (Millbay Docks) in the annual Associated British Ports report.
WESTERN MORNING NEWS,
10 April 1985

G.W.R. liner tenders							
Name	Official number	Built	Tons gross/net	Dimensions (ft)	Engines	At Millbay	Disposal
Sir Francis Drake (1) **Helper**	68324	1873 Preston Iron	173/59	131.3 x 20.1 x 10.0	2cy. Diag. Paddle	1873—1910	Sold Weymouth
Sir Walter Raleigh (1)	74618	1876 Preston Iron	151/47	110.1 x 19.1 x 10.0	2cy. Diag. Paddle	1876—95	Sold South Shields
Palmerston	44923	1864 Cubitt Town Iron	109/55	96.5 x 18.5 x 9.4	2cy. Simple lever Paddle	1883—1913	Sold Newcastle
Smeaton	86510	1883 Preston Iron	369/200	125.2 x 35.1 x 11.1	Compound Twin screw	1883—1929	Sold Belfast
Sir Richard Grenville (1) **Penlee**	97475	1891 Birkenhead Iron	420/103	132.0 x 30.1 x 12.6	2cy. Comp. Twin screw	1891—1931	Sold Dover
Cheshire	97754	1889 Birkenhead Steel	387/59	137.2 x 28.0 x 11.4	4cy. Comp. Diagonal Paddle	1905—13	Wrecked
Sir Francis Drake (2)	124571	1908 Birkenhead Steel	478/168	145.8 x 38.6 x 14.1	Trip. expan. Twin screw	1908—53	Scrapped 1954
Sir Walter Raleigh (2)	124572	1908 Birkenhead Steel	978/169	145.9 x 38.6 x 14.1	Trip expan. Twin screw	1908—47	Sold France
Atalanta	124469	1907 Dundee Steel	577/57	170.3 x 32.2 x 15.3	132 n.h.p. Twin screw	ex LSWR 1910—23	Sold South-ampton
Sir John Hawkins	161262	1929 Hull Steel	939/359	172.5 x 43.1 x 14.6	Trip. expan. Twin screw	1929—62	Scrapped Holland
Sir Richard Grenville (2)	162909	1931 Hull Steel	901/338	172.5 x 42.7 x 14.7	Trip. expan. Twin screw	1931—63	Sold Jersey

Port Health Authority launches						
Name	Period in use	Built of	Length x Beam Draught (ft.)	Crew	Engines	Speed
Clytie	1915 to 1929	Pitchpine and teak	28.0 x 8.6 2.0	2	1915 12 h.p. 1920 12 h.p. Kelvin 1929 18 h.p. Kelvin sleeve-valve	(1) 6 knots (2) 7 knots (3) 8 knots
Golden Hind	1929 to 1949	Pitchpine on oak frames	50.0 x 12.6 3.5	3	60 h.p. Kelvin petrol/paraffin	9 knots
Argus	1950 to 1981	Mahogany on oak frames	40.0 x 10.0 3.0	2	1950 Thornycroft diesel 1966 Tempest diesel	

Ocean Mails Express — 9 May 1904		hr.	min.	sec.
Millbay Ocean Terminal	dep.	9	23	10
Plymouth North Road	pass	9	26	17
Newton Abbot	pass	9	59	52
Exeter St Davids	pass	10	22	12
Whiteball Tunnel	pass	10	41	41
Taunton	pass	10	50	01
Bristol (Pylle Hill avoiding lines)	arr.	11	26	29
Bristol (Pylle HIll avoiding lines)	dep.	11	30	12
Bath	pass	11	43	50
Chippenham	pass	11	56	00
Swindon	pass	12	09	49
Didcot	pass	12	29	20
Reading	pass	12	42	21
Slough	pass	12	55	15
Paddington	arr.	1	09	58

Salvage Vessel Artiglio II						
Name	Official number	Built	Tons	Dimensions (ft)	Engines	Based Millbay
Artiglio II ex **Mauritaine** ex **Catherine**	1687	1908 Blassentils Nantes	386	152.5 x 24.9 x 13.1	58 h.p.	1931—4

Research vessels						
Name	Built	Tons Gross/Net	Dimensions	Engines	Owners	At Millbay
John Murray ex **Noblesse**	1963	441/80	133.6 x 25.9	2 x 394 h.p. diesels 11.5 knots	N.E.R.C.	1967–71
Shackleton	1954	1658/276.7	200.5 x 36.0	785 n.h.p. 10.5 knots	N.E.R.C.	1971–6
Discovery	1962	2321/661	239.5 x 46.0 x 23.4	Ruston-Hornsby diesels	N.E.R.C.	1976–7

Port Officer's launch, Board of Trade					
Name	Official Number	Built	Dimensions (ft)	Engine	At Plymouth
Gadfly	132769	1919 Tignabruaich Wood	40.5 x 8.6 x 3.9	Paraffin motor 26 n.h.p.	1921–30

Bibliography

The Blue Riband of the Atlantic Tom Hughes (Patrick Stephens, 1973)
British Shipping R.H. Thornton (Cambridge University Press, 1945)
Daily Star (Files)
The Egypt's Gold D. Scott (1933)
Exeter Flying Post (Files)
A History of Plymouth C. W. Bracken (SRP Ltd, 1931, 1970)
Mercantile Navy List (H.M.S.O.)
Plymouth & Devonport in Times of War and Peace H. F. Whitfeld (Chapple, 1900)
Plymouth: A New History Crispin Gill (David & Charles, 1979)
Plymouth: A Portrait J. C. Trewin (Robert Hale, 1973)
Port of Plymouth Review (Files)
The Railway Magazine (Files)
Red Rocks of Eddystone Fred Majdalaney (Longman, 1957)
Sea Breezes (Files)
Shipping Wonders of the World Clarence Winchester (Fleetway House, 1936)
Ships Monthly (Files)
Southampton Echo (Files)
Western Morning News (Files)